The Black Excellence Project at Bard Early College D.C.

Book Editors
Cassandra J. St. Vil, Ph.D.
Michael J. Sigrist, Ph.D.
Jonathan R. Freeman, Ph.D.

Project Partners
Amateka College Prep
U.S. Department of State
Partners of the Americas
4.0 Schools
and undoubtedly,
the brilliant founding scholars
and supportive families of
Bard Early College D.C.

The Black Excellence Project and "BEP @ Bard"
is brought to you by the partnership and collaboration of
Amateka College Prep and Bard Early College D.C.
Both of these organizations are at the service of
Washington, D.C. students and families
to escalate academic and social success.

The Black Excellence Project is funded by
the Citizen Diplomacy Action Fund for U.S. Alumni;
a small grant program sponsored by the
U.S. Department of State with funding provided
by the U.S. Government and administered by
Partners of the Americas.

History took on a different meaning, because it was no longer "Read this bland passage, memorize this vocab and answer these questions". You really cared about what we as students had to say, and you made sure we always had a place to say it.

-**Jailynn Brown**

Learning amid COVID-19
Spring 2020

"BEP @ Bard" Foreword

A thought for today.

I am super angry. I think anyone with a conscience should be super angry. In the words of James Baldwin, "How much time do you want for your progress?" is a question I hear in my daily thoughts, when I read people's comments, when I hear my students talk about their struggles, when I speak with my students, etc. I am angry that so many people are comfortable enough to ask those who are uncomfortable to wait just a little longer for progress. I will focus on speaking more constructively because I agree, people need to simmer in the message not just react to the boiling water.

So, I ask all who read this:

How much time do you want for your progress?

Because we can't wait much longer and truly, nobody should have to wait. We have proven in the last few days and weeks just how immediately change can occur if the gluttons will kindly step out of the way. Thank you, James Baldwin.

When we study the past, we often read about the narratives of darkness and desperation, the big events that marked an era. What is much harder to convey than names and dates is the general spirit of the times, how life had no choice but to go on amidst the uncertainty and anxiety and sadness.

Often moments of tragedy are brought on, or at least exacerbated, by our hubris. We as humans can be blind to what threatens us. But we are resilient. This resilience, however, is not passive. It requires us to come together for ourselves and others, even if we are physically separated. Read and watch the news. We cannot or should not hide from the truth of what is taking place. But also remember, that is not all there Is to life.

We are left with a lot of time to sit and think. That is the nature of this particular crisis. The news is grim, and will likely get grimmer. But there is still joy and hope. There can be. There must be. We have scientists working on treatments and a vaccine. We have businesses improvising. We have people thinking of how they can help. Along the way, we cannot forget that to be human is to be a mix of many emotions and instincts. So please find ways to nurture the breadth of life. As we fight for the future, let us make sure we bring along the beauty as well as the pain.

This moment in time is historic.

The entire world is feeling the impact of the widespread Coronavirus (COVID-19) in one way or another. Despite our temporary isolation in the wake of a global pandemic, a diverse group of students at Bard High School Early College in Washington, D.C. continued to work effortlessly on this important anthology highlighting and celebrating the significant contributions of African-Americans who have worked toward racial justice in their respective fields. entertainment, music, scholars, entrepreneurs, etc.

The Black Excellence Project at Bard High School Early College or "BEP @ Bard" achieved its goals to:
increase reading and writing proficiency,
affirm Black identities and local Black history
and recognize student's voices.

The Black Excellence Project is sponsored by Amateka College Prep, an organization working to celebrate Black communities in Washington, D.C. schools. BEP @ Bard Project Partners include the U.S. State Department via Partners for America, and 4.0 Schools.

Jonathan R. Freeman, Ph.D.
Historian and Co-Editor
Amateka College Prep

Table of Contents

Page Student Voice

4   Foreward
9   Project Background
11 The Black Excellence Project Essay Guidelines

14 Damari Thompson
16 Yahrie M. Queen
19 Qalei Coles
21 Abraham Outtara
23 Taylor J. L. Allston
25 Micora Cogdell
27 Khalisa Brown

32 Ebony Adams
34 Chanel Hawkins
36 Patience Verene
39 Jayden Hickman-Richardson
42 Cayleigh Johnson
44 Jacaree Proctor
46 Karin Bishop

51 KeVonte Perry
53 Kyla Johnson
55 Ava Pitcher
58 Katelyn Shanks
61 Adonias Stuckey
63 Zoi S. Anderson
65 Leah Mallard

70	Amoree Richards
72	Rakaya Irving
74	Kiarah Smith
77	Armon'e Green
80	Desteni Waters
82	Mya Martin
86	Da'Rell Massey
88	Kamiah Hopkins
89	Wynter Jackson
93	No El
96	Epilogue
98	Afterword
100	Acknowledgements

Project Background

A nationally renowned academic model providing its culturally diverse student body with college-level coursework and credit taught by a reputable faculty, Bard opened its doors in August 2019 as the newest high school campus within D.C. Public Schools. Our initiative, "BEP @ Bard" provided literacy-instruction to the founding class of 9th grade students of Bard Early College D.C.

BEP @ Bard was created by Amateka College Prep to expose students to historical and contemporary Black figures who have made an instrumental impact upon Washington, D.C. to raise awareness of these topics and increase commitment to the city. Examples of these figures include, Chuck Brown (musician), Ralphe Bunche (diplomat), Frederick Douglass (abolitionist) and Mary McCleod Bethune (civil rights activist) to recent D.C. notables, Taraji P. Henson (actress) and Trayon White (city councilmember). Course topics studied local Black leaders from a variety of fields, demonstrating multiple college and career pathways as avenues for success and social impact.

Bard Early College's national network, as well as, Washington, D.C. is culturally and racially-diverse, including a large presence of Black residents and students. Our project invites students from all racial and cultural backgrounds to develop grade-level literacy skills while engaging with exemplary local Black figures to learn from. Race, racism and countering anti-Blackness is rarely spoken of, let alone taught, among multicultural groups. Our project delves into social justice and identity work to promote cross-cultural community among D.C.'s high school students.

Together,
Cassandra St. Vil, Ph.D.
Faculty of History, Bard D.C. &
Founding CEO, Amateka College Prep

along with,

Michael Sigrist, Ph.D.
Faculty of History, Bard D.C.

The Black Excellence Project
Essay Guidelines

PROMPT: Write an essay about Black Excellence <u>addressing the guiding questions below.</u> Your essay must be **at least 5 paragraphs** in length, and include introductory and conclusion paragraphs. Each paragraph must be at least 5 sentences long. Use the recommended questions to help expand your writing. This assignment can be typed or handwritten.

DUE DATE: Monday, March 16, 2020 IN CLASS.

<u>**Select essays will be chosen for official publishing!**</u>
Write your best work and in neat handwriting. Remember to check for grammar and spelling.

Write at least one paragraph each to answer the following guiding questions about Black Excellence:

1. **What does Black Excellence mean to you?**
    - Why is it important to learn about Black Excellence?
    - Do you believe it is important to learn in schools? Why or why not?
        - Where, other than school, do you learn about Black Excellence?
    - *How* do you want to learn about it at school?
        - Should it only be taught in certain subjects? For instance, should it only be learned in history class?
        - What would you expect in math and science to celebrate Black Excellence?
2. **Who is an example of Black Excellence?**
    - Choose anyone that we learned about at school. This can include individuals we studied or people you know (teachers, family members, coaches, etc.).
        - What are the most significant aspects about this professional's background?
        - What is their professional pathway?
        - How did they use their career to fight racism?

- Why are they an example of Black excellence?
3. **Who else is an example of Black Excellence?**
    - Choose anyone we didn't get to learn about. This can be an individual or group of people (i.e. Michelle Obama, Regina Hall or Black scientists)
        - Who else would you want to learn more about? Why does it matter to learn about this individual or group?
        - How are they an example of Black Excellence?
4. **Are you *"for* Black Excellence"?**
    - How do you (or, will you) show your support of Black Excellence?

In your conclusion, please address:

- How would school or life overall change if we celebrated Black Excellence?

What does Black Excellence mean to you?

Who is an example of Black Excellence?

Who else is an example of Black Excellence?

Are you "*for* Black Excellence?"
How do you show your support of Black Excellence?

How would school or life overall change if we celebrated Black Excellence?

Damari Thompson

Black Excellence to me means that one or more people that performs on an expectation higher than standard that can be taught to other people older or younger. Black Excellence means alot to me, it is taught in so many ways through people, classes, situations etc. A lot of things would not be here if it weren't for the people who represent Black Excellence and I dislike that some people take it for granted. It's a very important and critical subject that should be taught in all schools no matter what class. Black Excellence is not only an important and critical subject it's also a very disturbing subject to talk around certain people, some people may be offended in some ways depending on if their race is brought up in certain stories from the past. I learn about Black Excellence a lot outside of school. My Grandad teaches history at another school and he makes me learn more and more about it every single time I go over his house. Some schools don't teach Black Excellence at all and I have issues with that, how can you leave a very important part of all history out of all of the brains of the students who aren't taught it?

Kevin Durant is a great example of Black Excellence and he shows it in various ways! Kevin Wayne Durant is a professional Basketball player who now plays for the Brooklyn nets, Kevin was born on September 29, 1988 in Suitland, MD he is currently 31 years old and has plenty more basketball to play ahead of him. When Kevin was younger he used to do photography outside of playing basketball and enjoyed it alot it was in fact one of his favorite hobbies. Kevin grew up around an area called Seat Pleasant with his mom it was just him and her, that was an inspiration for him so he strived and strived and kept believing in himself and on from there look where he is now. Kevin to me is a great example of Black Excellence he teaches people that anything you put to your mind you can achieve including your goals etc.

Another person who is a great example of Black Excellence is Maya Angelou, she also shows how she is an example of Black Excellence in plenty ways. Maya Angelou also known as the "Queen of Poetry" was an American poet, singer, and memoirist and Civil Rights activist. Maya was born on April 4th 1928, in St.Louis, Missouri and raised in St.Louis and Stamps, Arkansas. Maya became one of the most renowned and influential voices of our time, with over 50 honorary doctorate degrees. She became a celebrated poet, educator, dramatist, producer, actress, historian, filmmaker, and so much more! Maya is a great example of showing Black Excellence she tells and inspires people through all of her work with so many different things and lessons of her work teach you.

I am most definitely for Black Excellence. I would support it in every way I know how to. Black Excellence is a very large and wide subject to learn about and I am just starting and I know that for a fact, over these next four years of high school I will continue to learn, love, and definitely support this movement of Black Excellence. To whomever reads this essay I hope I inspired you to explore and learn more about Black Excellence maybe someday you'll be a great example of it.

Yahrie M. Queen

Black Excellence Project

Black Excellence means to celebrate the remembrances of important people who make the Black community proud. It's important to celebrate the achievements and goals of the Black community because our ancestors used to be slaves. As slaves, we wanted to find a way to be free and achieve equal rights. It was very rough for black people to get an education and have the same rights and privileges as Whites. Mainly, White people had greater opportunities than Black people. White people were viewed as being upper class, whereas blacks are considered lower class. Black Excellence, also means to stand up for what is right, protecting your community, standing up for others, and being a role model for kids that do not have anyone to look up to.

Someone representing Black Excellence in my family is my great-grandmother. My great-grandmother represents Black Excellence because she was born in 1931 and faced a lot of troubles in her life. She is currently 89 years old, and will be 90 on September 24, 2020. This proves that she went through hard times by fighting for her rights. She also lived through World War II and The Great Depression. One thing I have realized is that food was much cheaper back then. During 1963, on August 28th, my grandmother participated in a march in Washington, DC advocating for Jobs and Freedom. During this time it was very difficult for African Americans to get jobs or have free opportunities, and my grandmother decided to fight for these important causes.

Another person who represented Black Excellence was Dr. Martin Luther King Jr. Dr. King was born in 1929, but died in 1968. Dr.King decided to become a spokesperson and a Civil Rights Movement leader from 1955 to 1968. Martin Luther King wanted to speak up for himself and others because he felt the current laws were unfair and racist. This is another reason why we celebrate Dr. King in the month of February, during Black History Month.

I am for Black Excellence because I am a black young lady and stand up for my country to make all actions fair. I am a type of young lady that values fairness. If I were to show support of Black Excellence I would speak and ensure that everyone in the entire United States has access to free education, employment , housing , and parents have access to money to adequately support their children. It is important to support "Black Excellence" because it shows how many people actually care about other peoples' lives and how generous a person can be.

If schools celebrated Black Excellence it would be a positive because school is a community. Celebrating Black Excellence at school can make the school a safer place to be. Students, teachers, and staff would feel more comfortable being in a place where everyone could come together as a whole and understand and support each other. If a person felt unsafe at a place that they attended 5 days a week , they would not want to return. In order to feel comfortable in a space you have to adapt to it. Life would change overall because everyone would adapt to the new type of community and everything would be different, in a good way. There would be fewer killings, less homelessness, and people could take better care of their family because they would have better income. . As a consequence of these things, I am thinking of becoming a spokesperson just to make the world a better place.

Qalei Coles

Black excellence is being able to push through adversity. I think it is important to learn about Black Excellence because I feel that black people do not receive the right amount of attention for intentionally making the world a better place. It is important to learn about black excellence in schools because not only do white people achieve greatness in the world, many African Americans have achieved similar greatness and deserve respect for their contributions too. For example, Taraji P Henson grew up in Washington, D.C., was rejected from the Duke Ellington the School for Arts for acting, however she is a well known actress and has starred in many well known on screen titles, such as "Empire" and great movies like "Hidden Figures".

I live with black excellence. I am reminded every day what it means to be for Black Excellence. Black excellence is my mom. I believe we should be taught black excellence at school in courses like literature, history, art, and dance. If Black Excellence were taught in Math and Science I would expect to learn about African-Americans who formulated math equations that solve world problems.

Kevin Durant is another excellent example of Black excellence. Kevin Wayne Durant is an American professional basketball player for the Brooklyn Nets of the National Basketball Association. He played one season of college basketball for the University of Texas and was selected as the second overall pick by the Seattle SuperSonics in the 2007 NBA draft. He currently plays for the Brooklyn Nets and produces a TV show named "Swagger". He uses his career to fight racism by funding money to black schools, communities, and organizations. He even created a basketball court in Washington, D.C. for black communities in the area. Kevin Durant is an example of Black Excellence because his father left his family before his first birthday. Life got difficult for Kevin, his older brother Tony, and his mom. However, Kevin Durant found a way to keep persevering with life through basketball. He honed his basketball skills to the point where he made it into college and eventually was drafted in 2007 to NBA Seattle SuperSonics. He lived a hard life and although his family and life had challenges, he still found a way to keep striving and became one of the greatest NBA players in the league.

  I would like to learn more about Zaya Wade. It is important for me to learn about Zaya Wade because I find her to be an awesome example of Black Excellence. She stopped living as someone others wanted her to be and became what she wanted to be. It's inspirational because not many people would have the courage and confidence to do what she did at age 12. She inspires other people to be themselves. Zaya Wade flaunts who she is and loves herself.

  I intend to show support for Black Excellence by trying to become the best version of myself and follow my goals and dreams. In conclusion, if my school celebrated black excellence, yes, it would be informational, but it would also be great because most school events are overly boring. Therefore, I don't think it would change anything except make school more interesting. It would also make me, my friends, and most likely other people that really hate that day or week enjoy school during the time Black Excellence is celebrated.

Abraham Outtara

Wes Unseld Essay

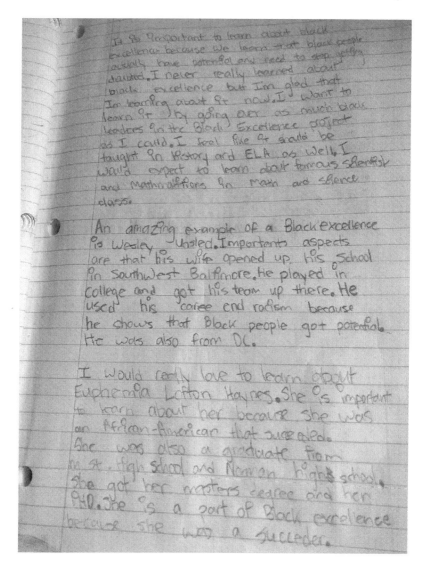

It is important to learn about black excellence because we learn that black people actually have potential and need to stop getting doubted. I never really learned about black excellence but I'm glad that I'm learning about it now. I want to learn it by going over as much black leaders in the Black Excellence Project as I could. I feel like it should be taught in History and ELA as well. I would expect to learn about famous scientist and mathmaticians in math and science class.

An amazing example of a Black excellence is Wesley Unsled. Importants aspects are that his wife opened up his school in Southwest Baltimore. He played in college and got his team up there. He used his caree end racism because he shows that Black people got potential. He was also from DC.

I would really love to learn about Euphemia Lofton Haynes. She is important to learn about because she was an African-American that succeeded. She was also a graduate from M st High school and Manan Heights school. She got her masters degree and her PHD. She is a part of Black excellence because she was a succeeder.

I show my support by working hard, staying in school and focused as a young African-American male. I am also studying on plenty Black Excellence leaders. I also am from DC and one day I'll be just like on of them if not better. I will also take every opportunity. I will go to college as well.

People would care more about black people. Black people would be more confident than they are. More black people would succeed. Black people would have potential than they already have. Black people are important.

Taylor J. L. Allston

Black Excellence Project

To me black excellence means a black person being the best person they can be. Black excellence means working hard to achieve your goals and getting back up when you get knocked down. We see black excellence everywhere, from rappers, singers, business owners, sports players, teachers, chefs, and artists. Black excellence is something that should be taught and shown everywhere because not only is black excellence beautiful, it is empowering to black children everywhere.

One example of black excellence is Dave Chappelle, who is an African American comedian who was born in Washington D.C. Chappelle uses his platform to bring light on social issues such as racism, drugs, African American culture, and human sexuality. Chapelle has worked on numerous projects and programs, including the Chappelle show, Robin Hood: Men In Tights, Undercover Brother, and many more. Dave Chappelle believes that people in the spotlight should be leading during this age of social activism. During Russell Simmons Rush Philanthropic Arts Foundation Chappelle told the audience "This is a very surprisingly emotionally charged time, so people like me, I think, are very relevant and necessary in sorting through all this information and emotional content, And when we are at our best, hopefully we are doing a great service to many people."

https://thegrapevine.theroot.com/dave-chappelle-on-activism-the-biggest-enemy-of-an-ar-1790886759

Another person who is an example of black excellence is J. Cole, a rapper who uses his platform to help and bring up other black musicians. One thing that he has done that is an example of black excellence is that he founded Dreamville Records. Through his recording label he has signed many aspiring black artists such as J.I.D, EarthGang, Ari Lennox, and Omen. J.Cole recorded an album titled Revenge of the Dreamers, where he features other black artists, some of which are unsigned, to create music and allow the artists to keep the rights to their own work.

I believe black excellence is very important and should be taught in schools to uplift black kids. Teaching black excellence will set black kids up to succeed in life, while also providing kids with role models to look up to. People can teach black excellence by teaching the history of black people and by showing more black representation in the classroom and in the world. One way I believe that I can show black excellence is by working hard to achieve my goals and by helping others achieve their goals.

Micora Cogdell

Black Excellence Project

Back excellence means wonderfully empowering African American people who have done amazing things that make the black community proud. It is important to learn about black excellence so you become aware of some of the greatest black people that ever lived and those still alive that continue to contribute to Black Excellence. Black excellence should be taught in schools to inspire millions of kids. Black Excellence can be taught through so many different subjects because there are countless black people doing so many amazing things.

Dr. Bernice Johnson Reagon is a person that represents Black Excellence. Dr. Bernice used music to set a strong foundation for the Civil Rights Movement through the use of freedom songs to build up the people. Her musical group "Sweet Honey in the Rock" used freedom songs to raise voices, empower individuals, and accomplish together what we cannot accomplish alone. Dr. Bernice is an example of black excellence because she inspired so many people to stick together for change.

I would love to learn more about Taraji P. Henson. I would want to learn more about her because she started from the bottom and now earns a six figure salary as a Hollywood actress . I aspire to one day become an actress. People like Taraji P. Henson are an example of black excellence because there are not many black actors in a very white-washed business. Also she did not achieve success overnight; she studied acting at Howard University and began her Hollywood career in many guest roles until she got her first big role at age 31.

I am 100% for Black Excellence because I one day want to be a part of the black excellence as either an activist, journalist, entrepreneur, or actor. I will also show my support for Black Excellence by staying close to my culture and religion. I will also learn as much as possible about Black Excellence. and inspire myself to be a better person.

Khalisa Brown

Space and Stem - Black Excellence in Women

Black excellence is the never ending legacy of barrier breaking and accomplishments achieved by black people. Everyday things like traffic lights, peanut butter and even door knobs are the products of black excellence. Black excellence should be a cornerstone of American education, especially in predominantly black areas of the country. I think this project is perfect for Bard DC, a Ward 7 school, because it encourages us students to breathe life into our dreams. Not only in history class, but also in ELA, math and science, because many breakthroughs in these fields were achieved by African Americans and other people of color, but are often ignored or discredited. Learning about our history in all classes, not just black history, but excellence from all cultures would be very stimulating, and could inspire students to be examples of excellence in general!

Mae Jemison is an excellent example of Black excellence in science. Jemison was born October 17, 1956 in Decatur, Alabama. She moved to Chicago at age three and cultivated passions for astronomy, anthropology and archaeology. She graduated from Stanford University in 1977 with degrees in Afro-American studies and chemical engineering and in 1981, a Doctor of Medicine degree from Cornell University. During her time in Los Angeles as a general practitioner, she and 14 others were selected by NASA for astronaut training. Dr. Jemison completed her training period in 1988 and became the first African American woman in space in September 1992. Her journey on the shuttle Endeavor left a remarkable legacy, long after she resigned from NASA in 1993. Not only did she break barriers during her mission, but Dr. Jemison formed the Jemison Group afterwards to expand a love of science in students and to market advanced technology in developing countries. She broke stereotypes of women in science fields, and represented black women as a force to be reckoned with in astronomy.

Another example of black female excellence is Marjorie Lee Browne, an exceptional mathematician and educator. Born September 9th, 1914 in Memphis, Tennessee, Browne grew up where advanced education and intellect was high priority. Her biological mother died when she was two, but Browne's father and stepmother encouraged her and her siblings to take full advantage of their education. She attended LeMoyne High School and graduated from Howard University in 1935. She became an educator in New Orleans, Louisiana at a school called Gilbert Academy, but relocated to Ann Arbor, Michigan a year later. She earned her masters and doctorate from University of Michigan in 1939 and 1949. Browne was only the third African American woman in her field to earn her doctorate! Browne returned to teaching, this time at North Carolina College, after receiving her PhD. She set up a computer center there in 1961, one of the first of its kind at a minority college. Marjorie Lee Browne earned many awards for her education throughout her career till she retired in 1979. Unfortunately, she had little time to enjoy her retirement, as she died on October 19, 1979. Thankfully her achievements live on to this day.

With these great examples to look up to, I show my support for Black excellence by studying and expressing my creativity in every way possible.

The whole purpose behind this movement is to educate and empower youth of color to see their full potential, so I try to put it to use every day by reading and writing. I am not sure what career I will pursue, so I do well to try everything brought to me. I really enjoy learning stories of Black excellence because it reminds me that I came from a great line of people, who have been degraded and discredited for their accomplishments. Exceeding expectations and knocking over obstacles previously set for me is my way of supporting and advancing Black excellence.

Reflection Page

What does Black Excellence mean to you?

Ebony Adams

The importance of learning about Black Excellence is to learn about amazing people and the wonders that they have done and continue to do in this world. It is very important to learn about Black Excellence in schools because some young folks prefer not to read books at home. Church is another place one could learn Black Excellence because Lord knows that some of these students need Jesus and need to be taught a good lesson. Teachers could try to motivate students to learn about fascinating things through the use of games involving Black Excellence or through the use of a poster board. Black Excellence could be taught through any subject, however it is ultimately up to the teacher to teach it. For example, math teachers could try to hide math equations inside of a photo or a drawing. Similarly, science teachers can try using science experiments to promote Black Excellence.

Taraji P. Henson is a great example of Black Excellence. She is an amazing actress, which is a significant aspect to her professional background. She earned a NAACP (National Association for the Advancement of Colored People) Image Award for Outstanding Actress in a Drama Series. Henson attended Oxon Hill High School in 1988, she also attended Howard University in 1995; but before attending Howard University, Henson set out to get a higher education at North Carolina A&T (Agricultural and Technical) State University. Henson studied electrical engineering at North Carolina A&T. She has starred in movies like *Hidden Figures* and *The Best of Enemies*, which helped fight racism by showing the world how black people as a whole were mistreated. Taraji P.

Henson's acting career has helped the black community. Taraji P. Henson is from D.C. and is thus aware of the struggles that us young people face living in the "hood." Through her story, we can learn how to overcome these challenges to become successful.

Another example of Black Excellence is Regina Hall. I would love to learn more about Regina Hall who is in a high-powered job, working night-and-day as a successful actress. Hall is a funny role model who has and still is doing great things with her acting career. This is why I would like to learn more about her personally, her acting career, and the life story while living in Washington D.C. Regina Hall and Taraji P. Henson are both from the Washington D.C. area, so they both understand the struggle especially in terms of overcoming adversity reaching the successes they have as great Black American women. The things that make Black Excellence important is understanding historical struggles, such as: racism, segregation, poverty, etc. These things teach us that if we can get through these struggles then we can get through anything.

I am all for Black Excellence because I support excellence in all races. I support Black Excellence mainly because I do not hate on my own skin color, regardless whether they are tall or short, young or old, annoying, or immature. I am proud to be Black. We as a whole, have the potential to do anything we set our minds to. We work hard for what we want, even if others think it is only a dream. That is really the only difference between greatness and the "haters" of the world. Black Excellence and the Black Community will succeed not only because I believe; but because I am also Black Excellence.

Chanel Hawkins

I'm Black and I am Proud

Black excellence isn't just one person or one thing; we all symbolize Black Excellence every day.

Black Excellence can be found in someone who is black and portrays great qualities and abilities that make the black community proud. To me, Black Excellence is displaying strength and dignity.

Those who display Black Excellence portray great qualities and are leaders. For so long black people were put down; Black Excellence means doing the opposite. Black Excellence means embracing your blackness and uplifting other African Americans.

Taraij P. Henson is an example of Black Excellence because she shows what it means to be a black woman. From rags to riches her story has inspired people all across the globe. Her talent and impact are inspiring.

Gabrielle Union is another woman who exemplifies Black Excellence. She is an advocate for women's rights and for the LGBT COMMUNITY. Her voice helps other black women and men stand up for what they believe in.

For so long black people have been portrayed as something we are not, so having good leaders helps us to be confident in who we are.

Showing my respect for Black Excellence means being the best person I can be. One way I can do this is to stay in school and begin to establish myself in the world. I hope by becoming who I want I can inspire others around me. I want to be just like or better than the inspiring people who came before me. I will respect my blackness by protecting it and nurturing it.

In conclusion school or life would change because Black Excellence would touch more people. I believe that black people deserve to be celebrated. We have contributed a lot to the world and will continue to do so. I'm proud to be back and I wouldn't want to be part of any other race. We should feel proud and not ashamed of who we are.

Patience Verene

Black Excellence can mean various things to many people. To me, Black Excellence is Black people working together, as one, to strive for greatness. Black Excellence is smiling through any situation no matter how hard and painful it is. Black Excellence is never giving up on your dream. Black Excellence is about being bold, unique, strong, and brave. It is about not being afraid to step outside the box. Black Excellence is Black teachers teaching Black students how to read and write well. It is when teachers teach them Black history. It is when teachers teach students in general. Black Excellence is you.

Many people portray Black Excellence in different ways. In order to show Black Excellence, sometimes you have to go through a major life experience . An example of such a person that bounced back in a tremendous way is musician Chris Brown. Chris Brown was born on May 5th, 1989 in Tappahannock Virginia. He is a B.E.T. Billboard, and Grammy award-winning musician. He is also a father of 2 children. However, he experienced some bumps in the road on the way to becoming great. Unfortunately, Chris Brown was involved in a domestic violence incident with another award-winning artist, Rihanna. In 2009, Chris Brown went to jail for physically assaulting Rihanna. Long story short, he became one of America's most hated celebrities for assaulting Rihanna. This situation and his music career incidentally helped with racism because he is half Black. Many White people wanted him in jail. Instead of giving up he fought for his rights as a musician and as a human to not be placed in jail. Although he went to jail, things were still complicated for him. Chris had a major support system that was helping him get out of jail in a safe and non-detrimental way in order to preserve his music career. He was eventually released from jail and then things started to look better. After years of work and perseverance, he became one of America's most loved celebrities. He had a daughter in 2014, and a year later he dedicated an album to her and named it after her. In 2019, he had a son. Things typically didn't start to go right for him until he had his daughter. He has released 4 albums since the birth of his daughter . He portrays Black Excellence by working hard and changing people's perception about him so that he can continue to do what he loves, creating music and providing for his family.

Another way people show Black Excellence is through the use of music. One person that does this without a problem is Mario. Mario is a two-time Billboard winner, born on August 27, 1986, from Baltimore, Maryland. He shows us that Black love is amazing and if you really love someone or something, then you must work hard for it. He fought against racism by showing us that all races could love each other. He shows that no matter what you go through music can bring you together. He shows us that Black Excellence is not only shown in business or fame, but it is also within us and our hearts.

Just like many other people I know, I support Black Excellence. I support Black Excellence because it could mean many things. It could mean being bold, or it could also mean entrepreneurship. It could mean happiness, or it could mean love. I support Black Excellence because many people think you will be unsuccessful due to the color of their skin. That is not the case as long as you are confident and you have faith in yourself that you will succeed, and show Black love everywhere you go.

If schools or people worldwide celebrate Black Excellence the way it is supposed to be celebrated then I think the world would come to a better understanding of what Black Excellence is, to the point where people would love to be around each other. To the point where no matter what disagreement we have we should be able to bounce back and work together to be better as a whole. Overall Black Excellence is beautiful and I am here for it all the way.

Jayden Hickman-Richardson

Black Excellence

To me Black Excellence is when a person of African-American descent helps people in any way, is successful, becoming successful, and/or working on bettering themselves. It is important to learn about Black Excellence because African-Americans as a people did and still do face many hardships and it is a beautiful thing when a person of African-American descent who has been discriminated against and wronged jumps all the racial hurdles they have been faced up against and succeed in life and usually the people who are able to jump those hurdles are great and capable minds.

I believe Black Excellence is very important to learn in schools. It molds young impressionable minds in a positive way and gives them a role model that is heavily needed in present times with all the bad influences around.

Learning Black Excellence in schools also helps kids of color learn how they should go about the discrimination they are shown and have a good and successful life. Other than school I learn of Black Excellence from the news outlets and social media and I think it is good that they push that type of information. In school I would like to learn of Black excellence by having (in an allotted amount of time and not interrupting any other learning) a Black Excellence day where students indulge in activities that further their knowledge of Black Excellence and are given a giant history lesson. I believe history class is the best place to learn about Black Excellence if it didn't cut into any other learning. If Black Excellence was taught in a class other than history it should be something that still falls into the subject being taught. If Black Excellence was celebrated in math or science I would expect to do an equation or an experiment about something the person who's accomplishments they are celebrating.

Frederick Douglass is a great example of Black Excellence. The most significant aspect of his background was that he was a slave. Frederick Douglass' pathway to his career as an social activist and an abolitionist was learning how to read and write. Frederick Douglass was a leader in the abolitionist movement and was on the front lines of the fight on racism. He gave speeches letting people know how incredibly wrong the practice of slavery was and was a big presence in abolitionist meetings and plans. Frederick Douglass is a good example of Black Excellence because he was a very intelligent black man who helped to end the slavery of his kind.

Michelle Obama is another great example of Black Excellence. Michelle Obama is a successful lawyer and university administrator. She also was the first black First Lady and is married to the 44th President Barack Obama. Somebody else I would like to learn more about is Dr. Mae Jemison. Dr. Mae Jemison is an example of Black Excellence because she is a very intelligent and successful black woman.

I am Black Excellence. I am an example of Black Excellence because I am working on bettering myself and being successful. We already learn Black Excellence in school to a certain extent. If we celebrated it more people would know more successful black role models to follow after. Black Excellence should be celebrated because black people faced and still face a lot of hardships but we should also celebrate and educate other minorities and other people that succeeded through a lot of hardships.

Cayleigh Johnson

BEPS   Cayleigh

1: It is important to learn about Black Excellence because there are alot of Black figures that many students don't know about. There are alot of figures that have helped the Black Community that many people in DC don't know about. We also need much more people helping the black community.

- Black Excellence is so important to learn in schools. Many americans don't know how many African Americans have affected the world, neither do some students in DC. They don't know how much the world has been impacted by Black Excellence.

- I barely learn about black Excellence and that's a big problem. That's why it needs to be taught to students all around the world, today and until society improves.

- It should not only be taught in history class, it should be taught in ALL classes.

2. Benjamin Banneker was an example of Black Excellence. He was an author, surveyor, naturalist, and farmer. He had little to no education and was self taught. He had knowledge of astronomy. He conversed with Thomas Jefferson about the topics of slavery and Racial equality. Benjamin demonstrated that Black people were capable of things such as scientific and technological achievements. Many people also refer to him as the "first black scientist."

Born in Baltimore, Maryland.

3. Another example of Black Excellence is Jacqui D Henson. She attended Howard University. She also won the Golden Globe Award for Best Actress in 2016, for her role in Empire.

4. I will show support of Black Excellence by telling many people I know about African Americans that helped improve society.

Jacaree Proctor

It is important to learn about Black Excellence because of the impact African Americans had on people and the country they lived in. Black Excellence is very important and should be taught in all schools across the country because of their many accomplishments throughout history. You can learn about Black Excellence on the Internet, on social media, or even from our own families at home. I want to be able to learn about Black Excellence through the Internet because it gives us a fun way to be able to learn and we are more used to the Internet so it would be more comfortable. It should be taught in every class because an African Americans contributed to every subject in some way. I would not expect for them to teach it but if they mentioned some African Americans who helped in creating the things we use to explain the way we think.

Edward Kennedy "Duke" Ellington is an example of Black Excellence because of his contribution to the music industry during the great depression. Ellington started playing the piano at the young age of 7, and in 1932 he dropped the most popular songs during the Great Depression and he was one of the five Black people in the world to ever make the cover of Time magazine. During his career Ellington was a musician, pianist, composer, and leader of a jazz orchestra. Ellington used his career to fight racism because he was a black man succeeding at a time when black people were still being put down. He often mentioned racism in his songs. Duke Ellington was one of the most popular musicians of his time and his music has changed many things about the music people listened to.

Barack Obama is another example of Black Excellence because of his contribution to his country. It is important to learn about Obama because he was the first African American President of the United States of America and he has an interesting backstory. Obama is an example of Black Excellence because of his many accomplishments as a black male such as becoming Illinois state senator, U.S. senator from Illinois, 44th President of the USA, and was awarded the 2009 Nobel Peace Prize laureate.

I am for Black Excellence because African Americans have been put down for centuries so now that they have "equal" rights we should celebrate the accomplishments they've done Black Excellence is important because it gets to show off how African Americans have done many great things despite being oppressed for most of history. Learning about Black Excellence can empower young black kids to try to do amazing things like the many great black people have done or try to be better than them. Also, African American children would be comfortable with learning about it because it lets them learn about people who look like them.

Karin Bishop

Black Excellence

Black Excellence is a form of celebrating or recognizing the accomplishments of Black people.

      It is a way for Black people to get the recognition they deserve. It is important to learn about Black Excellence because it gives people from other races, including even Black people, a chance to become informed of the accomplishments Black people have made and the ways in which they have affected or changed our lives. Learning about Black Excellence in schools is important because it gives black people a chance to have the spotlight which they hardly have. Other than school, I learn about Black Excellence on award shows like the BET awards or the NAACP awards. I would love to learn about Black Excellence from a Black person or from someone who is an example of Black Excellence. Black Excellence should not only be taught through subjects like history. It is bad enough that Black people do not get the recognition that they deserve, only learning about Black successes in a single class is unfortunate. We can, for example, in subjects like math and science, celebrate Black Excellence by using methods discovered by Black people to solve problems and perform experiments.
      My father is an example of Black Excellence. My dad is an HVAC department manager for Jiffy Heating and Plumbing. However, he had to work his way up to get that position. He worked in the field, took multiple classes, and earned degrees. He is now a manager and

helps guide young workers in the HVAC field. The most significant aspect about his professional background is that he learned how to be more of a leader than he already was and he devoted his time to multi-tasking because he has to watch everyone.

My dad is the only Black manager and one of the few Black people that work there.

My dad is an example of Black Excellence because he not only used his time to help others at his job but he also gives young boys and his children advice about life. He teaches us how not to make the same mistakes he did as a teenager/young adult.

Angela Bassett is an example of Black Excellence because she is an African-American actress well known for putting forth her best effort in movies and showing lots of emotion. She is the first African-American to win a Golden Globe Award for Best Actress in a Motion Picture Musical or Comedy. Angela Bassett is important because she is an example that Black women could do the same and achieve as well as whites or mainly White women. She is an example of Black Excellence because she shows young Black girls that you could make it in Hollywood (and in life) if you just believe and do not let people get in the way of achieving your dreams. One of her quotes are "The world has white people and black people in it. Even in Harlem." This quote stands out to me because she shows that the world is diverse and you might see unfamiliar people in places they normally wouldn't be and that didn't stop her from making it and achieving her dreams.

I am definitely for Black Excellence. I believe that Black Excellence should be celebrated everyday based on the pain Black peoples have been through for hundreds of years. I will show my support by taking time out of my day to actually show my appreciation for what Black people did or went through for me to live the life I'm living today. Also, I would recognize how hard Black people worked to make their way in industries that were not always used to Black people. Black people have worked extra hard to make a way in this world and thanks to the ones who came before me they paved a way for me to become successful in this world.

If more people celebrated Black Excellence in schools, and life overall, we would have massive change. If Black Excellence was brought to the attention of other races discrimination and racial profiling would stop. People would stop seeing Black people as an automatically bad or guilty person if they realize all the good that had been done by us. Crimes committed by Black people are more likely to be talked about rather than crimes by White people. That is why we, as Black people are immediately judged. If Black Excellence was televised as much as crimes committed by us then the world would change for the better.

Reflection Page

Who is an example of Black Excellence?
Who else is an example of Black Excellence?

KeVonte Perry

To me...Black Excellence is someone in the Black community who possesses or possessed great traits that made the black community what it is today. It is important to learn about Black Excellence, especially if you're also a part of the Black culture and community. The History of Black culture comes with important figures that did great things, from the power of speech by Martin Luther King Jr., to the humongous charitable donations of Lebron James. Black Excellence should be taught by more than one subject. Black Excellence came in many different arts and cultures. For example, Ray Charles (1930 - 2004) showed Black Excellence by the work and art of music, even with the loss of eyesight. Mae C. Jemison became the first Black astronaut to travel into space. In my eyes and point of view, I think Black Excellence should be taught in every subject, and more importantly for history, music, and science.

Black Excellence has many great African-American figures in the community. An example of one is Dr. Evelyn Boyd Granville. Granville was the second African-American woman to earn a Ph.D in mathematics and helped in America's early space missions. She helped fight racism by giving away here incredible knowledge to the next generation of mathematics and all schools. She became known as an example of Black Excellence due to her accomplishing something special for the community, while also being African-American.

Another example of Black Excellence was Kelly Miller. Miller was the first African-American to attend John Hopkins University. He spent his time studying mathematics, physics, and astronomy. Miller was also a member of the Alpha Phi Alpha fraternity. He taught mathematics at the M Street High School in Washington, D.C. Miller also graduated from Howard University in 1903. He's an example of Black Excellence because he never gave up on his education as a black student at an all white college. He showed that anybody could do so.

In the future, I plan to be for Black Excellence because I want to provide charity to my community. I not only want to use the riches of my music for cars and big mansions, but I also want to share my riches with my (Black) people. I can relate to the struggle of my (Black) people and I do not want them to go through the same struggles I had to go through. I do not want everyone in my community to feel the pain of struggle.

If we were to celebrate Black Excellence, I think it would wake the world up. I think it would wake the world up because people of the Black community would understand why they should not kill each other. I think people would start to realize that everybody has a dream and doesn't want it to end. If we were to celebrate Black Excellence, the world would be way different.

Kyla Johnson

Learning Black Excellence is essential because it shows us good role models and people we should want to be like as we get older. It is important to learn Black Excellence in school because we could do projects and very intense research on black figures. Learning about Black Excellence outside of school would also be significant to younger generations. Learning about Black Excellence should not just be taught in one subject or only in schools. There are many successful Black actors, artists, mathematicians, scientists, and professors. Every class should talk about Black Excellence at times.

An example of Black Excellence is Gabrielle Union. She is an American actress, voice artist, activist, and author. She uses her career to fight racism by giving job advice to people who have experienced racial slurs, racist jokes, etc. She has even experienced racist slurs and jokes from when she worked on America's Best Talent. She is an example of Black Excellence because she is a successful Black public figure who is a great role model.

Another example of Black Excellence is Beyoncé. She is an American singer, songwriter, record producer, dancer and actress. She uses her career to fight racism by encouraging brown skin people to step out their boundaries and do what pleases them no matter how people feel about it. She even created a song called "Brown Skin Girl" feat Saint Jhn, and Wizkid and Blue Ivy carter. She is an example of Black Excellence because she encourages a lot of people to do what they enjoy, she also shows people the outcome of how it feels when you do what you enjoy.

Am I for Black Excellence? I am for Black Excellence! I love Black Excellence and I think it is a good topic to talk about with all ages. We have so many underrated Black women, men and children with so many great talents. Black Excellence should be talked about more all around the world not just in schools or when there is a racial issue.

If Black Excellence was celebrated it would have a big impact on a lot of younger Black generations. It would celebrate all the Black figures that have been successful and do things for the Black community. It should take place in February just like Black History month. It would be a time for recognition that African Americans are part of a long, proud, profound, and difficult history. We've also contributed to all parts of American society.

Ava Simone Pitcher

Black excellence isn't just achieving your short and long term goals, it's different levels such as breaking barriers, making a difference, being successful, and making history.

No matter how long it takes, don't give up on something if it's important to you.

It is indispensable to include Black excellence in schools and to announce the achievement of African Americans. Including Black excellence in schools allows the new generation of students to learn from their mistakes, follow in their footsteps and set pragmatic exemplars. Black excellence teaches young African American men and women to appreciate and cherish themselves because in this world anything is possible. In many parts of the world there are historic sites to expand your knowledge when it comes to black history such as libraries, museums, and memorials of civil rights leaders.

Euphemia Lofton Haynes was born on September 11th, 1890 and died on July 25th, 1980. She was the first African American woman to receive a doctorate in mathematics at Catholic University of America in 1943. Later in 1959, she joined the District of Columbia Board of Education and became president of the organization in 1966, this allowed her to continue her fight against racial segregation. Haynes earning her Ph.D was shocking because men believed that women should not have educational rights. She inspired not just African

Americans, but women around the world to strive towards their goals in life. When Haynes died in 1980, the Catholic University of America inherited $700,000 from her real estate.

    Benjamin Banneker was born on November 9th, 1731 in Ellicott's Mills, Maryland. His father Robert was a former slave and his mother was Mary Bannaky. Since Banneker's parents were free slaves, he was able to escape. Benjamin was self-educated and highly intelligent, he was capable of learning and teaching himself astronomy, solar eclipses, and prognostication lunars. From 1792-1797 Benjamin published multiple almanacs that obtain astronomical computations. In 1791, Banneker wrote a letter to Thomas Jefferson hoping that the letter would gain support from him and look at African Americans as equals rather than slaves. Banneker scolded Jefferson and his followers for their moral standards for enslaving African Americans. Benjamin published his letter to Jefferson and his response gained political support from the audience and press as well, this increased the widespread assistance of abolitionists across the country. Benjamin Banneker later died on October 9th, 1806 as an ensured racial equality activist writer.

    Many people in the world support and demonstrate Black Excellence by attending events such as "Black Lives Matter," supporting black owned businesses for example gathering together to watch a play performance, watch black owned films, starting peaceful protest throughout the streets and neighborhoods they call home, help raise awareness by throwing a party or cookout, or spreading the success of someone's hard work or foundation.

Society, schools, and everyday life could change if we celebrated Black Excellence by encouraging one another to love, believe, and keep pushing forward to reach your desired goal. If we had nothing but love, without killing, without jealousy, and without greed, there wouldn't be a world full of people with hatred buried within their hearts. Love, Respect, and Discipline are the three key rules to life.

Katelyn Shanks

The Black Excellence Project

Black Excellence to me means when people of color succeed whether in history or modern times. Learning about Black Excellence in school is very important. Learning about it can inspire children to do things that can benefit themselves and their communities. In school, through history books and speakers who have contributed to Black Excellence, will be the best way for students to learn about it. I believe that Black Excellence can be taught in every class. There are people who have contributed to Black Excellence that are mathmaticians, scientists, physicians, actors, lawyers, and much more. Since these people are not only historians, so Black Excellence should not only be taught in history. In math and science, I expect mathmaticions and scientists to celebrate Black Excellence.

Kelly Miller is an example of Black Excellence. Miller was born on July 18th, 1863. At age 23, he graduated from Howard University in 1886. Miller became the first Black man to be admitted to study at Johns Hopkins at age 24 in 1887. At age 26, Miller finished his post-graduate work in 1889. At age 32, he became the first to teach sociology at the university in 1895. Miller recieved his masters degree in 1901 at age 38.

History Class

Learning about Black Excellence is important because it can inspire young African Americans to want to do something can can contribute to it. Learning about Black Excellence in school is important because thats where you can reach children the most. You also learn about it in muesoum. I believe that you can learn about Black Excellence in all subjects. In math and science, Black Excellence is celebrated by acknowledging the work done by mathmaticians and scientists.

Madam CJ Walker is an example of Black Excellence. She started out as nothing and was able to help build the confidence in all black women in her time. She was even able to give them jobs paying more than what they made at first. Madam's hair growth serums allowed women of darker color feel equal to those of lighter complexions. She is an example of Black Excellence because not only did she help end racism, she was able to help women of color get better paying jobs all over the country.

Another example of Black Excellence is Taraji P. Henson. Taraji ~~oooo~~ is a good example because despite her past, she became a well known actress. She contributes to Black Excellence because she recieved outstanding awards such as the "NAACP ~~oooooo~~ Image Award for Outstanding Actress in a Drama Series." I believe that Taraji P. Henson is a great example.

I will support Black Excellence by ~~con~~ donating money to small black owned businesses. My school should celebrate Black Excellence because many students may be inspired to contribute to Black Excellence in their own way.

Adonias Stuckey

Black and Excellent

Black Excellence is very important for the African American community. Black excellence means a person that is an example for colored people, they are what young African Americans can look up to as a role model and leader.

It is important to learn about Black excellence in schools because we are trying to uplift the black community and change the stereotypes and stigmas.

An example of black excellence is Kevin Durant, Kevin is a professional basketball player. He plays for the Brooklyn Nets but is currently injured. Kevin injured his Achilles playing last season for his previous team the Golden State Warriors. Kevin Durant is an example of Black excellence because he is an African American that has gotten to the NBA. He is a great player and is proving that no matter who you are, you can overcome obstacles just like his injury.

Another example of Black Excellence is Martin Luther King Jr. He is a great example of black excellence because he showed people that African Americans were not violent or disrespectful. He showed that he can be calm, resilient and loving, showing all of the different thoughts about African Americans. He was a preacher, taught about God and how to show everyone love even if they don't do the same. He was no hypocrite and a prime example of his words of wisdom. He used his preaching and virtues to fight segregation peacefully even though he was not receiving the same treatment. He was an example of black excellence because he showed everyone what African Americans can be and he was an African American at their best.

The black excellence project is a great idea and I think everyone can contribute to making it even more outstanding. I can support black excellence by being myself, an example of black excellence.

Show people not to read a book by its cover and surprise everyone with the content within that book.

As a result, the black excellence project can change a lot of lives including mine. This can and will change a lot of opinions on young black people. My life will change, doing this I will have a better view and understanding of the fact that I can be anything and I will be more motivated to be what I want.

Zoi S. Anderson

Tony Lewis, Jr's Impact on Washington, D.C.

Black Excellence....to me it is a person or a group of individuals that are educators for the black community. Individuals who are willing to give back to their community because they want to guide and lead their people to be successful and great. These individuals do not contribute to their communities for fame, credit, or money. Black Excellence is important to learn about because we need to acknowledge the people who created history, who gave us a voice, faith, and the mindset to do it all again but bigger and better. We need to be aware of black educators that are teaching us not to wait around like fools, but to get up and make a mark in history.

Learning about Black Excellence in school is important to talk about because we NEED to know who started the evolution in the past and who is continuing it now. School is not the only place I learn about Black Excellence. I also learn about it at home, my mom and I talk about starting a business and about how we can inspire the black community. Black Excellence should be one of the main topics that we learn about in school because we don't talk about it as often as we should, all we ever hear about is slavery and black people working for "The Man." We don't have discussions about self-employed black people working together, building each other's self-esteem, or being each other's positive influence. Black Excellence can be included in all aspects of academia. There are many historians, mathematicians, scientists, and other black professionals that should be included and studied in school.

Author, local activist, ex-offender counselor, outreach worker, advocate for children with incarcerated parents, and the son of the District of Columbia's ex-kingpin, Tony Lewis Jr. is a community leader who has fought tremendously over the past sixteen years to uplift and empower men, women, and children impacted by mass incarceration. According to https://www.dmvlife.com/tonylewisjr.html, Tony Lewis Jr. has dedicated the last decade of his life serving the underserved in the District of Columbia. He has primarily worked with the at-risk youth and ex-offender populations from a workforce development perspective.

In 2010, Lewis founded Sons of Life, an outreach organization that provides social and educational programming to children with incarcerated parents. Sons of Life works to keep inmates connected with their families by providing transportation to prisons. They also organize clothing and toy drives for families of the incarcerated. In November 2010, Sons of Life partnered with international recording artist, Wale, to give away more than two hundred Thanksgiving dinners to families with incarcerated loved ones. Lewis did not focus on racism, he focused on bringing men, women, and children together with their families. He is an example of Black Excellence because his mindset is focused on bringing families together no matter the cost. He also wanted to redefine the way other people thought of him. All his life he was known as "the kingpin's son" but when he started giving back to the community and helping families that changed.

Leah Mallard

Black Excellence in My Community

Black Excellence to me is, black people positively contributing to the black community and inspiring other black people to do the same. Black Excellence teaches everyone that black people are not stereotypes. Black people are worth more and can do more than what many people assume. Learning from examples of Black Excellence is important because black people aren't praised about enough. Most of the time, people that are celebrated in history for their work are white people. Black people deserve to get their accomplishments acknowledged because we have to work hard and go through societal barriers to achieve them. Learning about Black Excellence doesn't always happen in the classroom and it should never be restricted to being taught in certain subjects. Learning about influential black people should be incorporated into every subject. In subjects, like science, we should regularly learn about black people like Mae C. Jemison or Otis Boykin. Their names should be as common as Einstein or Newton, we deserve to be acknowledged.

An example of Black Excellence is Evelyn Boyd Granville, She was a scientist born in the District of Columbia in 1924. In 1945 she graduated Summa Cum Laude as one of the top students in her class. But she didn't stop there; she got her Ph.D in mathematics from Yale University. In 1962, she began working as an analyst for NASA. Her work there is what she's most famous for, Granville's mathematical calculations helped land a man on the moon. Though at the time she was less appreciated for her work, we can now acknowledge that her work was spectacular. Equality was not a norm for women in the workplace let alone a black woman. After NASA, Dr. Boyd Granville was an educator to 8th graders and college students until 1997. Dr. Boyd Granville is a perfect example of Black Excellence because she is a black female scientist who helped land a man on the moon and also taught black children that they too can do the unimaginable.

Another example of Black Excellence is Carter G. Woodson, he was an author, journalist and historian born December 19, 1875, in New Canton, Virginia. He was the second African American to earn a doctorate from Harvard University. He dedicated his life to educating black people about their history and encouraging us to get our thoughts and ideas recognized. He also advocated black history to be taught in schools. Over the years his program gained more support and is now recognized as Black History Month. Carter G. Woodson is an example of Black Excellence because he seeked the best education possible to share his knowledge with his community.

As a black female I feel very strongly about Black Excellence and supporting other black people who break barriers and do the unimaginable. I am going to support Black Excellence by supporting other black businesses and teaching other people about the importance of our strength. I will also become a doctor and accomplish the unthinkable so I can show other aspiring black doctors nothing is beyond your reach if you really want it. Black Excellence is everywhere and we have to show the world what we can do. If everyone celebrated Black Excellence the world would think differently. History would be more inclusive and there would be less questions and looks of surprise when people find out that black people didn't only invent peanut butter. We would talk about the other parts of our history aside from slavery and the Civil Rights Movement. We would have a more complete knowledge of our history and where we came from. Everyone would know how much we really contributed to today's society. Now, our mission is to spread Black Excellence so everyone will know about the black kings and queens that made a difference. We would have a voice. We would be heard.

Reflection Page

Are you *"for* Black Excellence?"
How do you show your support of Black Excellence?

Amoree Richards

To me Black Excellence means everything to me. Growing up being an African American male in the whitest state in the USA I was never ever able to experience Black Excellence that much because there weren't many examples presented to me. But when my mom decided to move to Washington, D.C. my vision of Black Excellence broadened greatly as I saw all of the amazing creations of African Americans. After spending many years in Washington, D.C. and growing in knowledge, I can finally witness and participate in Black Excellence.

Someone I know very well that is an example of Black Excellence is Kevin Durant. Kevin Durant is an African American NBA all star that was born in Maryland, he is very successful. Because of his success, he donated money to different programs in the DMV and gave back to his community. He didn't leave his community and just take care of himself, he returned and made contributions to his community which I believe is a characteristic of Black Excellence.

Someone I know from my day to day life that represents Black Excellence is my mother. She was devoted to moving my sister and I into a better environment surrounded by people who look like me to show me that I can achieve whatever I want. She talks about giving back to communities and how it affects everyone around you. Even though she may not be able to give to her community, she gave back to me and I can hopefully fulfill her dreams and give back. I never would've known of Black Excellence if it wasn't for her.

Everyone should be aware of Black Excellence and understand how it has impacted the world. If they do not become aware, individuals will continue to be white washed and negate the contributions of Africans Americans to society. Black Excellence needs to be studied in schools and acknowledged throughout the world to become a societal norm.

When I was younger, I was unaware of what Black Excellence meant. After being exposed to what it stands for, I now believe in and am for Black Excellence. When I am older, I want to give back to numerous communities so they can experience Black Excellence and understand how it can greatly affect others. I want to stand out to the world as an African American that made a difference. I want to be a face of Black Excellence so I can educate others. I am Black Excellence.

Rakaya Irving

What Black Excellence Means To Me

Black Excellence, to me, means African Americans showing their many great abilities. It also means uplifting each other and influencing people in the black community to achieve their goals. Black Excellence is important because it makes a huge impact on people's lives. I believe it is important to learn about Black Excellence because it can inspire young black students to be successful in life and learn about other people in history that represent Black Excellence. I want to learn about Black Excellence in school by relating the subject we are taught to black leaders, it should be taught in all subjects. Black contributors to math and science, like teachers, should be represented in Black Excellence.

Elizabeth Catlett is an example of Black Excellence. She highlighted the struggle of African Americans with her art as a graphic artist and sculptor. She is an example of Black Excellence because through her art she explored themes relating to race and feminism. She is an African American woman who positively influenced others through her art and sculptures.

Kevin Durant is an example of Black Excellence. Durant was born on September 29, 1988 in Suitland, Maryland. I would want to learn more about him because he plays professional basketball and inspired me as a little kid to play basketball. Kevin Durant is an example of Black Excellence because he is a black NBA player and entrepreneur. Kevin Durant is a two time NBA champion and NBA finals most valuable player. He partnered with Nike and created his own basketball shoe. Kevin Durant's net worth is $170 million. His Black Excellence influences young basketball players in my city to be great and progress to play professional basketball.

  I am for Black Excellence. I know I am for Black Excellence because I'm a young black student that has goals in life ready to change the world. I show Black Excellence by doing magnificent in school and being dedicated to important things in life. I support Black Excellence by wearing black entrepreneurs' clothing in the DMV. For example, I wear a brand named "EAT" that was founded by a black entrepreneur.

  Black Excellence means African Americans displaying abilities that we can all achieve. Elizabeth Catlett, Kevin Durant, and many others represent Black Excellence. The more influencers we have the better the impact there will be in future Black Excellence achievers. I am for Black Excellence and will always be by succeeding and showing people that you can do anything if you put your mind to it. Education and life would change if we celebrated Black Excellence by influencing young black children and other races to have the desire to be successful.

Kiarah Smith

Black Excellence Through My Eyes

When you hear Black Excellence, a lot of ideas might come up for you. A lot of thoughts from the past, present, future, and memories of Black people, White people, and Hispanic people might come to mind.

Black Excellence can mean a lot. Black Excellence to me means proving yourself as a Black individual. Black excellence is being proud of your history and culture.. Black Excellence is believing that where we come from matters, my family and my life all matter. For a long time, Black people didn't really have the confidence and luxury to dream. Though we had the ability, we didn't have examples to look up to. An example that looks like us with curly hair and dark skin. We couldn't find beauty in ourselves to reflect our talents.

Learning about Black Excellence can be beneficial and is therefore important. For me, hearing that a Black person achieved something great is like hearing my brother or sister went to college. Not everybody feels that way about other people's success. Learning about Black Excellence in schools is good, but I don't think it's important due to the fact not everybody cares about Black Excellence no matter the race, and like other things you don't use it in your everyday life. Black Excellence can be taught in different ways, not just in school. You can learn by going to museums, using the internet or even asking people questions who know about Black Excellence. A person that represents Black Excellence in my eyes is Taraji P. Henson. This Black Woman is from Southeast, Washington DC and that is where I'm from and live. For a very long time, people used to say "nothing good came out of Southeast" and some still say it toda, but Taraji is one of many examples of the good that can come out of D.C.

Taraji is an American actress and author. She studied acting at Howard University. In 2011, she got her big break starring in John Singleton's film, "Baby Boy" and also plays a starring role in the popular show today, Empire. Taraji is very successful in what she does and a lot of people look up to her.

Another Black person that represents Black Excellence is Steve Harvey. Steve Harvey is an American stand-up comedian, television host and businessman. Before Steve became all these great titles he was once very poor. Steve was so broke at a point in his life that he had to live in his car for 3 years. Since childhood, Steve imagined being on TV. Growing up he went through a lot of bad situations.

Steve got humiliated by his teacher because she didn't believe in his dream, as he had a bad stuttering problem. After all this, Steve didn't give up on his dream; it actually made him stronger and helped him dream bigger. Steve has several television shows, but one of my favorites is Family Feud because it's funny and brings families together. Family Feud is a diverse show. Steve demonstrates Black Excellence by giving back to the Black community and being a lead example for everybody.

I am for Black Excellence. I show this by supporting Black individuals, whether it's watching their shows or movies, buying tickets to games or concerts, reading their books or poems, and sharing about them. I am happy for all Black Excellence. School and life would change day by day if we celebrated Black Excellence because it will give Black people hope who have trouble finding it. And it will also give everybody hope across all races. Meaning no matter where you come from it's not how you start it's how you finish and one day we will all be and feel equal and will be celebrating all Human Excellence.

Armon'e Green

Black Excellence is knowing your past, your surroundings, and the color of your skin and being proud. Using that knowledge to put good into the world. Tyler Perry and Will Smith, are two examples of Black Excellence. They are great African American actors who were raised very differently.

Tyler Perry was born on September 13, 1969. His childhood was very hard, and traumatizing for a child. He suffered from verbal and physical abuse. He was molested by three men, and a friend's mother. He became suicidal and was also homeless. Tyler Perry did not complete high school, but he earned a GED. These life challenges only made Perry stronger. At age 22, Tyler Perry financed his first play using his life savings. This was just a start, he had to maintain multiple jobs and was living out of his car. From 1998 to 2000 his play ' I Know I've Been Changed' was finally liked by critics and was staged at many places. The next play he came up with 'I Can Do Bad All By Myself' in 2000, was an instant hit. Also, his famous role, Madea played a huge role in launching his career. Another accomplishment of Tyler Perry's most famous film 'Diary of a Black Women ' budgeted $50.6 million. Tyler Perry showed Black Excellence by not letting his past dictate his future, instead of taking the sad, and easy way out he decided to persevere.

On September 25, 1968, Will Smith was born. Will Smith was raised in a happy home, as the oldest of four other children. He was raised in Wynnefield, Pennsylvania. His family stressed that education did not end when school ended, learning was continuous. Smith was 12 years old when he met Jeffery Townes, also known as DJ Jazzy Jeff, at a party. When Smith began rapping, he called himself "The Fresh Prince", he worked alongside DJ Jazzy Jeff, they were both successful. He earned a million dollars before the age of 20. He received his first grammy in 1988 for Best Rap Performance with DJ Jazzy Jeff. He also won the Blockbuster Entertainment Award in the favorite actor category for Independence Day, Men In Black, and Enemy of State. As many others have, Will Smith never displayed himself as someone with a turbulent background to gain sympathy from his audience.

    I am for Black Excellence. I show Black Excellence everyday by proving racist, sexist, and colorist people wrong. I pursue education, so I can become successful. I strive to be a person who shares talents, happiness, and success. If schools celebrated Black Excellence everyday, not just Black History Month, many kids would feel proud and comfortable in their own skin. They would know that they can be whatever they choose to be.

BEP @ Bard Instructors, "Dr. Mike" and "Dr. Cass" hang our banner up at the Bard Early College campus in Washington, D.C.

February 2020 – Michael Sigrist and Cassandra St. Vil are Bard faculty in History & Social Sciences.

Desteni Waters

It's important to learn about Black Excellence because it can help a young black child gain confidence in his or herself. It is important for African American students to learn about Black Excellence so they can understand how black people play an important role in every industry. African Americans have made many contributions to Poetry, Music, Dance, Art, Comedy and many other subjects. Young black students can find Black Excellence anywhere, if not in school then a library or a museum, or even in their family. Black Excellence can be taught in various subjects but it's mainly talked about in history. Black Excellence should be taught in subjects like math or science to learn about the successes of African Americans scientists, pathologists and other black academic professionals. Some people misunderstand the concept of Black Excellence, it is meant to be an inspirational historical ledger of the achievement of African Americans. It helps black children understand who they are and how special it is to be a black person. To teach young African Americans that the color of their skin does not define how intelligent and exemplary they are.

An example of Black Excellence is a DMV Rapper named YBN Cordae. In most of his music he talks about where he came from and how he was raised. DMV Rapper YBN Cordae expresses the pain of his violent upbringing in his art and music. Although he had a tough upbringing, YBN Cordae still managed to create music that any race could relate to and understand. At such a young age, it is admirable for YBN Cordae to be an inspiration to other young African Americans and an example of success.

I am for Black Excellence because it is proof that African Americans encourage one another to do well and have bright successful lives. I show my support of Black Excellence by continuing to learn about African Americans through education in subjects such as History and English and Black culture. Celebrating Black Excellence in school is changing the mindsets of young black students. Once students begin to learn about successful black people, they start to grow confidence in their own capabilities.

Mya Martin

Black Excellence

One who wishes to traverse the deep and complex history of those with African descent will often find themselves perplexed. From slavery, to wars and racism, the Black experience is no walk in the park. To this day, Blacks continue to fight an unfair battle for equal opportunities and rights. However, for that reason, it is critical that we recognize every moment where a Black person[1] has successfully pushed past their dark past. We recognize every time a Black person has exhibited Black excellence.

To have executed Black excellence means that a person of African descent has lived out the rights or opportunities they are deserving of despite[2] any racial barriers. While most people are given a small dosage of black history, much of the modern day experience is excluded. For example, in America, every child who attends school is required to learn about slavery. Some children are retaught slavery in multiple grades.

However, no child is required to learn the strides made today. Everyone is conditioned to learn about a time when Blacks couldn't even talk without permission.

Additionally, despite leaving an outstanding impact in several spaces, Black history rarely leaves the history classroom. Being a Black person who attends primarily Black schools and has lived in primarily Black communities, I'm surrounded by Black excellence in and out of school, but not everyone has the same privilege.

By ignoring Black excellence, nothing can improve.

A great example of modern day Black excellence is Taraji P. Henson. Born September 11th, 1970, Taraji would become one of the most well known Black actors today. Taraji attempted to pursue an engineering degree from North Carolina A&T University, but dropped out after not passing a math class. She held unsteady jobs for a while until obtaining her degree from Howard University in [3] 1995 and moved to Los Angeles. Taraji was consistently given small roles, until receiving her mainstream breakthrough in a movie called *"Baby Boy"* in 2011. From then, Taraji earned larger roles in shows and movies such as "Empire", "Hidden Figures", and "Tyler Perry's Acrimony."

Unlike most Black female actors who opted to play their roles safely, Tariji is often casted to execute her boisterous, funny, and blunt personality (often coming from Black female stereotypes). She acts out the life of a Black woman in realistic fashion. Her style of acting did not always attract or impress directors though. In her books and interviews, Taraji often shares the racist obstacles that have come her way from having a low salary to experiencing colorism when lighter skinned females often took her role. Despite such barriers, Taraji has persevered and continues to represent Black people and women alike, making her a figure of Black excellence.

Another exquisite example of Black excellence that most people don't know about is Ruby Bridges. Born in 1954, Ruby grew up in a segregated America, founded on the belief that Blacks and Whites could never be equal, and therefore never have the same privileges. Schools, water fountains, stores, and much more was segregated. After many years of fighting, the President launched an experimental program where select children would be allowed to attend all white schools. The first group, known as the "Little Rock Nine", was a group of teenage high school students. The first child to integrate an elementary school was a young black girl named Ruby Bridges. Everyday, Ruby was escorted by top tier law enforcers who protected her against racist teachers, mobs, and even the principal. Being only six years old at the time, one can only imagine how frightening the experience must have been. Ruby executes Black excellence through having the courage to endure every racist encounter that she did. Her small sacrifice set [4] the standard for endless black children who would later desegregate other all white schools.

For me, Black excellence remains a puzzling subject, despite my current knowledge. The past of many groups barely graze the complexity of black history. Teaching uneducated minds will not be an easy task in my opinion, but it should be taught. Just as when blacks did not receive equal rights, it was fought for despite the lives lost and[5] lives ruined. I stand for Black excellence because it changes people out of a mindset that Black people are weaklings who get taken advantage of left and right.

If said mindset was flipped and one could see a Black person as a survivor, rather than a victim due to Black excellence, many people would wear African descent with pride, a task harder than it should ever be for black folks around the world.

Da'Rell Massey

Black Excellence is important because, as a black person, it's important to learn about who you are and what your ancestors' have accomplished. It goes against the negative norm portrayed about African Americans. It is important for students to learn about Black Excellence in school to instill hope and inspiration. I believe it should be taught everywhere in all classrooms and subjects.

Wesley S. "West" Unseld is a former NBA player. He played for the Washington Bullets and in his first year he became Rookie of the Year and Most Valuable Player. Throughout his entire career he had chronic knee problems but was still considered as equally skilled as anyone else in the league. Before the NBA, he played for Louisville College and led them to three postseason appearances. He retired as a Hall of Famer and seventh all time in rebounds, retiring with 13,769 rebounds after 13 seasons.

Kevin Durant is a current NBA player. He is currently signed with the Brooklyn Nets. He played one season of college basketball for the University of Texas and was originally drafted by the Seattle SuperSonics. After playing nine seasons with that team he signed with the Golden State Warriors in 2016 and won back-to-back championships in 2017 and 2018. He is important because he is a great athlete and is a role model to other athletes. He dreamt about his success as a child and I dream of becoming a successful athlete as well.

Life would change if we celebrated Black Excellence because many would start to appreciate the accomplishment of African Americans. Individuals would see black people as an inspiration, more than just someone of a different race or culture. Everyone should start to celebrate Black Excellence because it will drive individuals to strive for greatness.

Kamiah Hopkins

To me Black Excellence means when someone black portrays great qualities also abilities that make the black community proud. It is important to learn about Black Excellence because it helps us succeed in life and continue our legacy. Yes, I do believe it is important to learn about ourselves in school because we can focus on the importance of historical Black Excellence earlier than the norm. I want to learn about Black Excellence by learning about it in history and advisory.

Anna Julia Cooper is an example of Black Excellence. The most significant aspects about Anna's background is that she was the daughter of a slave woman and a white slaveholder. Her professional pathway was advocating for African Americans in a respectful way. Anna Julia Cooper used her career to fight racism by becoming a popular public speaker. She is an example of Black Excellence because she paved a way for the black community to follow.

I would like to learn more about black women like Taraji P. Henson. Henson is an actress with roles in many black historical and inspiring movies. She is an example of Black Excellence because she is a powerful woman who started a nonprofit that addresses mental health stigma in the black community.

I will show my support of Black Excellence by uplifting and empowering my black community to strive for success and empower each other. We should be there for one another and stand by each other's side through hard times. School would change if we celebrated Black Excellence by bringing everyone together so we can start sharing ideas on how to protect our community and bring awareness to unknown issues.

Wynter Jackson

What Black Excellence Means to Me

To me Black Excellence can be used to describe any African American who is doing great things for themselves, the community or the world in general. We see lots of examples of Black Excellence in today's world and when we look at our history. We learn about Black Excellence In school, mostly during the month of February, which is Black History Month. We should be able to learn more about Black Excellence throughout the school year and in a variety of different classes. We learn about Black Excellence through history, and history can be incorporated into any class, so we should be able to learn about Black Excellence in any class. I believe we should.

One person who is a great example of Black Excellence is Langston Hughes. Langston Hughes was an African-American writer originally from Missouri. He lived in Harlem in New York for a while and even spent a few years in Washington D.C. Hughes wrote about the life of African Americans in his time period, what he experienced and the time periods in America before him. He was a leader of the Harlem Renaissance, which was an intellectual, social, and artistic explosion for the African American race. The Harlem Renaissance was centered in Harlem. Hughes wrote about this time period in forms of novels, poems and other writings. He was mostly known for being an innovator of Jazz poetry which is a form of poetry that incorporates elements of Jazz. All of his accomplishments are what make him an example of Black Excellence.

One example of Black Excellence in my life is my mother. My mother is a determined woman who is very caring and loves to help others. My mother sometimes works with the elderly and loves that work; she enjoys helping out the older people. She also loves to help out homeless people and the less fortunate. She inspires me to be the best I can be. This is why she is an example of Black Excellence to me.

I am for Black Excellence. I believe that everyone should be and can be for Black Excellence no matter what race you are. Being for Black Excellence just means that you are for black people doing amazing things, like reaching their goals and breaking barriers. I am for Black Excellence because I want to see my people strive for great things and achieve great things. Even if I wasn't Black I would be for Black Excellence. I show that I am for Black Excellence by supporting and showing love for Black businesses and black entrepreneurs. I also congratulate other African Americans when they show Black Excellence.

Every African American should strive for Black Excellence. Every African American should try to support Black Excellence and every other race as well. Anyone can be for Black Excellence no matter their race. You should be for Black Excellence because it might help lead to equality for all. And equality for all will ultimately make the world a better place.

Reflection Page
How would school or life overall change if we celebrated Black Excellence?

No El

True Excellence

Representing your community is part of what drives progress, and what allows the community to push forward. The roles of Individuals like Malcolm X and Michael Jackson in communities were controversial, but they gave their communities a sense of release from hopelessness.

Black Excellence is important because it is part of the entire pool of excellence, yet it is left out of the social norms of today. It should be taught in all schools because school is a place of educational development and by allowing students access to people of all cultures, they reach a complete level of education. It's important to avoid the rejection of inclusive academics; if nothing changes, we are forced to accept a white washed knock off of all history.

All academia should include the history of Black Excellence. It is unacceptable to say one subject should have it over the others. Since Black Excellence is present in all aspects of life, it should be included in every class curriculum. Especially math and science because the modern day math and science curriculum is white dominated. For example, everyone knows Neil Armstrong was the first white astronaut to land on the moon, yet no one has spoken about Mae C. Jemison, the first African American woman to travel to outer space. The fact that most people haven't heard of her makes it apparent that African American contributors are not acknowledged, which is unacceptable.

The most epic example of Black Excellence is one man who many people may not know about. He has devoted his life to the prosperity of those most hopeless, his name is Bryan Stevenson. He is the director of the Equal Justice Initiative in Montgomery, Alabama. He puts countless hours challenging discrimination in the justice system. He defends those who are put away forever, those who are innocent yet forgotten.

He is a role model that I look up to, because he lives the truth of seeing those most desperate for a voice. He motivates people to put work into the things that might not seem too promising. Students especially, can see him as an example of passion because students have to be committed to school, which is something that they might not be so sure about. Stevenson does this everyday. He is devoted to the redemption of those trapped in the hardest to reach crevices of the justice system.

In the book " Just Mercy" by Bryan Stevenson, he discusses his role in the Equal Justice Initiative as he fights for the freedom of a wrongly convicted man of color named Walter. Through this journey, Stevenson demonstrates how poor and under-resourced Walter's family was. It proves that without someone like Stevenson, the injustice in Walter's case would not be revealed. The book illustrates; the potential Stevenson sees in Walter, and their resilience to not give up.

Why Bryan Stevenson? Why Black Excellence? Without him, without it, there would be a piece of the world missing, a piece so inspirational, yet so hidden behind the world's current norms. Black Excellence, just like Bryan Stevenson, just like Walter, will never be forgotten.

Works Cited

Stevenson, Bryan *Just Mercy* 2014. Print.

Note: No El is an 11th grade scholar at Bard with connected commitment to celebrating Black Excellence.

Epilogue

I hope these essays inspired your thinking.

I hope they move you to action to create space in learning to recognize Black communities in schools.

Together, we decide not only *what* is important to learn, but *who* matters enough to learn more about in our studies. For centuries, we have been conditioned to believe that Black stories were not meant to be shared, that their narratives did not have anything to learn from.

Our students are learning from Black perspectives,

whether they, themselves are Black or not. In these pages, they've shared their voices, messages and opinions about what should be a part of their education and their place in this world. Their understandings of Black Excellence are as wide and diverse as Black communities are themselves. Are they 'African-American'? Or 'African American'? Of African descent? Dark skin? Light-skinned? Black or 'black'? Are we to learn about Black Excellence during the month of February or year round? In history or all classes? Do I have to be Black to be for Black Excellence? How does the world benefit from learning about Black excellence? What would be different if we finally celebrate Black heritage in our learning environments? Our students tackled these hefty questions, generously sharing their values, beliefs and attitudes with the public.

I have my opinions and certainly, my approach as I create these educational spaces where we all can learn from positive portrayals of Black communities. The mission of Amateka College Prep is to bring the voices of high school students to exchange ideas by reading and writing about the world's Black groups. We focus on adolescence at a critical time period when students are choosing who and what is important to them while discovering their own identities.

Our motto is to
Fill your space. Connect the World
where we invite students to share their thoughts, experiences and voices in order to uplift and bring people together. It is my hope that these essays charge you with the responsibility to honor student voice, seek local history and discover the many Black stories we can each learn from.

Connecting culture to curriculum,
Dr. Cass (Cassandra St. Vil)

Afterword

Dear Bard Scholars,

As I write this, we are still in the midst of the deadly Coronavirus pandemic while the centuries-long pandemic of racial injustice and police brutality rage on. While sequestered in your homes, you worked diligently in all of your subjects in a virtual format unfamiliar to most of us until March 13th and through all of the attendant hiccups, you persevered and shone.

As if the COVID-19 crisis and adjustment to virtual learning were not enough, you also endured viral video confirmation of the societal structures determined to confirm that your lives don't matter. But each of you, in your own way, have fought back. You have demanded time and space of us to process and grieve and plan. Some of you have taken to the streets to peacefully protest. Some of you are praying privately and in groups for the change you want to see in this world. Like the people you rightfully vaunt in your essays---famous athletes, authors, actors, doctors, activists--you, by #sayingtheirnames, by reminding the world that Black Lives Matter and that Breonna Taylor, George Floyd and Ahmaud Arbery embodied black potential and black excellence, you, too, are making a difference.

You inspire me. YOU are Black Excellence. I am so proud to know you and honored to have had the chance to read this book and to witness its creation. Thank you for being you and for sharing yourselves through this publication and all you do.

Sincerely,

Dr. Anderson

Vanessa Anderson, Ph.D.
Founding Principal, Bard D.C.

Acknowledgements

To the countless volunteers who reviewed essays, provided support and feedback to the curriculum and recognized the value of student voice and our mission.

Thank you.

The Black Excellence Project

Made in the USA
Columbia, SC
29 January 2021